/

I could not believe I encountered such an evil person. As I wrote this
book reminding myself of all the horrible different kinds of abuse I
put up with, it made me angry. Nobody deserves this kind of torture.
This book talks about my relationship with my child's father, a
covert narcissist. I had to tell my story. I had to get everything out.
Understanding narcissist abuse can be hard to understand especially
if you never experienced it for yourself. A lot of people think of
abuse as just being physical so that is why sometimes this kind of
abuse does not get classified as abuse when this kind of abuse can be
just as damaging as physical abuse. In this book I will talk about my
experience being in a relationship with a narcissist and I will point
out all of the different manipulation tactics and forms of abuse you
will experience when you are dealing with a narcissist. I will also
talk about the reasons I stayed so long and why I had to emotionally
detach myself from this relationship. If you were ever in a
relationship with a narcissist (or still dealing with one) and you read
this book, it is no doubt that a lot of the things you read will sound
really similar to your experience with the narcissist in your life. They
all use the same kind of tactics. A narcissist does more than break
your heart, they break your spirit. I used to think I was the problem. I
used to think maybe I was the crazy one and needed help like he
wanted me to believe. But once I started doing my research on

narcissism, I realized I was not crazy. I realized I was dealing with a psychopath.

I am a misanthropist so I already understood how evil and cruel humans could be. But this one really slipped by me. I never saw it coming. That is why I try not to let people too close to me because they usually end up hurting or deceiving me. This was my first real relationship with a man that was not just sexual. He was not my type. I was not physically attracted to him either. In the beginning he was such a sweetheart. He seemed so innocent, funny, and sweet. He has never been attractive to me as far as looks but I do not really care about all that. I cared about how good he made me feel in the beginning. I really thought he cared about me. I thought he loved me. He made me feel good and not even talking about sexually. I fell in love with him. I just knew he was the one and that we would be together forever. I always said I didn't think I would ever have kids because I couldn't see myself being with a man and going through that whole process of being pregnant and having a child but that changed when him and I got together. I saw how much he cared about his daughters and how he would talk to them all the time and I loved that. I love the way he interacted with his daughters and I wanted to have a child of my own with him and to start a family with him. I stopped taking my birth control so I could get pregnant by him. I told him the first day I stopped taking my birth control. I really do not remember what if anything he said. So, after five months of stopping my birth control, my period was one day late so I decided to take a pregnancy test and it was positive. I made an appointment with planned parenthood to get a test done with them and it also confirmed I was pregnant. I was so happy but still a little scared because I never been pregnant before or raised a child so I know it would be a new challenge, but I was ready. I could not wait to meet my baby. I did not know he was a Narcissist until after I had our daughter. Before the baby I noticed something was a little off, but I could not put my finger on it. It was not until after I started

googling his disturbing behavior, I found out exactly what he was....
a covert narcissist.

According to psychology today, "the danger is in not seeing through
the facade of a covert narcissist, because they're more passive. But
they can be just as destructive to relationships as the extroverted
types. The emotional abuse might be more silent and subtle but can
wear you down and demoralize you. Your needs and pleas for
attention will be discounted or ignored. You can get sucked into
trying to console and help this manipulative martyr to no avail.
There's no way you can fill their emptiness or change their victim
mentality. You're left feeling resentful and angry. Meanwhile, your
self-esteem is gradually undermined. The narcissist lacks empathy
for you, won't see you as a separate individual, and will do what's
necessary to maintain power and control. Their pain and needs will
always take precedence, so you're left feeling alone and neglected."

How I would describe my experience being in a relationship with the narcissist?

I was constantly walking on eggshells; they are overly sensitive and
angry so you must watch what you say to them or around them
because they will take it the wrong way. I could never express my
feelings or give my opinion or talk to him about what was bothering
me and if I did I got the silent treatment or got blocked or he got mad
and started screaming at me calling me all kinds of horrible names.
Narcissist lacks empathy. He did not care about my feelings. Any
conversation about how I felt ended up in an argument. Even when I
would try to talk to him as calm and polite as possible, it still ended
bad. He would even get mad at my facial expressions after he did or
said something to hurt or upset me. They are unable to see things
from other people's perspective. He felt he could tell me that my
feelings were "lies". He never took responsibility for his actions or
he would just twist everything around to be my fault. Narcissist are

known for gaslighting their victims. The constant criticism never stopped even when things were going well, he would constantly criticize me and call me names but could not handle any kind of criticism about himself. He would belittle me and point out every mistake of mines or flaw but could never see his own flaws or mistakes. He felt that all the problems in the relationship were 100% my fault and nothing was ever his fault. I went out of my way to please him and tried to make him happy and sometimes even put him before myself and nothing I did was ever enough for him. He was a big hypocrite; he constantly did things that he would have a problem with me doing. He never practiced what he preached. Communicating with a narcissist is like talking to a brick wall. They can ask their partners all kinds of questions and expect an answer but then if I would ask him simple questions like "do you work tonight" or "how was your day" he would just look at me and not say anything. That happened quite often. I never knew anything going on with him because he felt the need to tell everyone but me (i.e. he would plan trips out of town and didn't tell me, just randomly up and leave and not say anything, didn't know his work schedule and if I ask I would get no answer, etc. The only time I would know these things were if I overheard him telling someone or if it randomly came up later. But yet if he asked a question or wanted to know something simple like that, I would have no problem answering a simple question or I either already told him because that's simple basic communication in a relationship, something that he lacked. None of the problems in the relationship ever got resolved. It would either end in him giving me the silent treatment, blocking me, getting mad and screaming at me and not letting me get what I have to say out or I would just end up apologizing for upsetting him because I did not want to argue. He had the mindset of a child; things had to be his way or else. If he did not get what he wanted, or something upset him he would act very passive aggressive towards me to the point where the indirect aggression towards me was so obvious that I would ask him what is wrong or try to talk with him and he gets even more angry claiming there isn't a problem when clearly there is. He felt entitled to everything people around him had, especially money. He felt as if everybody owed him something. Anytime he knew I was getting some money from somewhere he made sure he got some but when he got his, it was only his. He would constantly try to project his bad qualities off on me when everything he would say was a true reflection of his self. And if I dared to call him out on any of his behavior, he would gas light me and twist everything around to make it seem like I am the crazy one with the problem and I am the one that needed help. I often felt unloved, unappreciated, and confused. He gave me mixed feelings. At first, I thought he truly loved me but then at times it seemed like he hated me. Sometimes he would come in and would not say anything to me at all. There would be no argument or anything, he just would not talk to me. Then the next day he would be talk to me as if nothing happened. Sometimes I would try to kiss him on his cheek, and he would be like "UGH" and sometimes I would touch him and he would brush my hand away from him as if he was disgusted and didn't want me to touch him. I never know which days would be the good days and which days would be the bad days. His mood swings would randomly change and whichever mood he was in, I had to act accordingly. It was an emotional rollercoaster. I never knew what was going to happen next as far as his mood swings. There have been days when he would come upstairs and interact with the baby and say nothing to me as if I were not there and then the next day he would speak to me or offer to buy me food and then maybe another good two days and then he is back to ignoring me as if I did something to him. I cannot understand how someone who claimed they love you would treat you like this. I got to the point where I started feeling so sick. Some nights I would stay up just crying trying to figure out what went wrong and why he was treating me so bad. He never felt any remorse. He did not care. Sometimes he was even amused and would smirk and mock me. Another thing Narcissist are very good at is they will do something so illogical or unreasonable to provoke a negative reaction out of you and then when you react to it or point it our they act like you are mentally unstable. The entire relationship is full of emotional manipulation. Narcissists are very sneaky, and they are pathological liars. He would lie about the smallest things that you do not even have to lie about. Even if you have clear evidence with facts and dates, they will still tell you that your facts are wrong and that you need help and that it is all in your head. These are very evil and dangerous people. And the worst part is, narcissist do not see anything wrong with themselves so that is why they never change. They just change victims. A narcissist would rather lose their partner than to fix themselves or admit they have a problem. Once you figure them out or you start putting yourself before them or they get bored with you, that is usually when the new supply comes into place. They do not replace you for someone better, they replace you for someone that does not know who or what they are. He told me before that if I am not happy then leave and go be with someone that makes me happy. These are heartless people. Instead of acknowledging the problem and trying to communicate like adults to fix our relationship issues, he would rather me leave so he never had to acknowledge any of his wrongs. It is easier for them to just get new supply and then they do the same thing with the new supply until they figure them out and that is why the narcissist has so many past failed relationships. These evil people will mentally and emotionally abuse you so bad to the point where you feel like you are going crazy and you start doing crazy things that are so out of your character. You stop trusting them because they are so sneaky and do not communicate with you and their behavior is so off that you just know something is going on. They will mess with you head and emotions in so many different ways then once they provoke a negative reaction out of you, then they start telling everybody that you are crazy, and you need help and that they are the victims and you are the abusive one. He told his family members, friends, and coworkers that I was the crazy one when all I did was react to how horrible he was treating me. Trying to make sense of a narcissist's actions will mentally drain you. Abusers do not abuse every day because if they did it would be obvious and that is what confuses a lot of their victims. Some days they have their good days but when things are bad they are extremely bad, and the scariest part is when you are dealing with a narcissist you never know which day will be good or bad. Another thing a lot of victims of this kind of abuse deal with is that abusers do not abuse everybody they encounter, so a lot of victims feel alone when trying to seek support from family and friends. The narc may seem so humble and cool in public but behind closed doors they are the devil and usually the only people who see this side are those that are close to them like a spouse. In the beginning you never see any of this coming because they are so sweet and seem so caring and they treat you so good and then once they get you hooked, that is when they start to devalue you and you see their true colors. That is when the mask comes off.

The Narcissist Description of you is Actually a Description of Them

The way a narcissist describes you is actually a description of themselves. They are very delusional. They use projection and if you pay close attention, accusations from a narcissist are really confessions. He would call me crazy, insecure, crackhead, retarded, thot, tell me I don't know what love is, etc. All of this is a description of him. He would call me crazy and insecure for pointing out his disrespect in the relationship. Narcissists want you to be blind to the disrespect and hurtful things they do to you and if you dare speak on any of it then they tell you that you are crazy and making things up and everything is all in your head. I was not insecure at all. There are just certain things you do not do out of respect for your partner, especially if you do not want the same things done to you. Crack head was a name he often called me. Not meaning that I was an actual crackhead, because I've never in my life done crack. It was just a way to make it seem like anytime I said something that he did not agree with or was not his perspective, then that means I must be on crack for thinking anyway other than the way he felt I should think. The same goes with retarded, anytime I said something he did not agree with or we had different opinions on, I would get called retarded. But if I were to get technical crazy and retarded would actually fit his description but normal people do not go around calling others hurtful names for no reason, especially their spouse. I was also often called a thot but that is exactly what he was. In his life he messed with some many women because he never had any standards. He would have sex with any female that showed him attention and was interested in him that way. He never had a type. He did not care if they were attractive, what size they were, what they had going for themselves, etc. He even admitted to having sex with every female unprotected, so he was the true thot. Narcissists are very delusional people. They lie so much, and they get to the point where they actually believe their lies. He said I lied about everything, but I always informed him on what was going on with me and tried to communicate with him and then he would brush me off and did not want to hear what I was talking about or either wasn't paying attention and then when I would bring it up later he would call me a liar and say I never told him. Everything he would accuse me of was actually things he was doing. He told me I would lie about going to work and be out doing other things when that was the farthest from the truth. At one point I even shared my location with him on my iPhone so he could see everywhere I went. I would also send him pictures of my lunch at work and talk to him on the phone before I would walk into work and text him when I was getting off just so he would not think I was doing anything. At one point I was even texting him letting him know if I ever left the office for anything like to go to the post office, or courthouse, or run an errand for my boss. I did all that so he would not think I was doing anything I was not supposed to be doing and so he would feel secure, but I still always got accused of doing things. If I were on the phone with him and I'm out at a store or somewhere and some holds the door for me, and I say thank you or I'm checking out and I tell the cashier thank you then he would automatically accuse me of flirting with them. He would often tell me I did not know what love was, but the ironic thing is, narcissists are incapable of love. They love what you can do for them and how they can benefit from the situation but as soon as you cannot give them what they want or you stop being their dummy, they no longer have use for you, and they move on so quickly to the next person because they never really loved you in the first place. You will give them your all and they will do nothing but drain you until there is nothing left. They feel like it is your job to please them and spoil them and you will barely get anything in return. They do not know how to love. They blame you for everything, they cannot communicate, they never want to talk and resolve any issues in the relationship, they never take accountability, they have a constant need for new supply, they take and barely give, nothing you ever do will be good enough for them, they play victim to circumstances they create and still find a way to blame the failed relationship on you. None of that is love. It is abuse.

"There is not true healthy communication and problem solving with narcissists. Narcissists run from confrontation because they do not want to take responsibility for their part in anything. They gas light and manipulate the conversation. They bring the focus back on you, by bringing up what you did wrong in the past. They get mad at you for getting mad at them. Anything to take the focus off of the, and avoid taking responsibility" – Maria Consiglio @understandingthenarc

"A narcissist does not want you to question their behavior, they want you to question your reaction. They tactically manipulate you into responding from a place of emotion so that you believe you are the problem. Your reaction to their abuse is labelled as abusive, irrational and crazy to remove any suspicion of themselves. This is called reactive abuse and it goes completely unnoticed by others" -Beth Watson @yourinnersherlock

"Narcissists don't want honest relationships, they want cheerleaders. They want people who always give them the right. They want blind loyalty. They want unconditional acceptance, no matter what they do. As long as you don't question anything they do, or give them the wrong on anything, they might just

leave you alone. But watch out, if you disagree with them, or go against them in any way. In their eyes, that is the deepest betrayal. And it never goes unpublished. Narcissists are spiteful and vindictive." — Maria Consiglio @understandingthenarc

September 30, 2020 was the last straw for me. I kept getting a very bad feeling about this one female co-worker of his. I noticed when it first started in March 2020 how he would be on the phone with her long periods of times, several times a day, several times throughout the week. And the only time these calls would happen was when I was not around. He never brought her around, never mentioned her or never introduced us to each other. At the time, his phone was in my name and I was paying both our bills, so I was able to see the call history. I noticed he was acting very different, so I decided to check the call history. They worked together during the same time and got off at the same time and would be on the phone with each other the entire ride home from work and he would hang up with her as soon as he got home. Or if I were at work, he would continue talking to her for a long period of time. It first became suspicious when one night I was at a family member's house and he was home and he had to work that evening but when I looked at the phone records I noticed that entire day he was on the phone with her for a long time that morning and almost that entire evening and the next day he said to me that he didn't get any rest because I kept texting him that evening. Not knowing that I saw the phone records from the previous day him saying that was suspicious to me. He didn't get any rest because he was on the phone with the girl the entire evening. So, I instantly knew then, it's something going on with this girl. And I felt like a fool because I paid for this phone and I was paying his phone bill for him to be constantly talking to the girl on my expense. So, I ended up blocking her number. And when I blocked her number, he got mad and started screaming at me saying mean things and calling me horrible names. So, I unblocked her, and he instantly started back talking to her. One day I looked in his phone and saw a text message from her saying good morning and asking was he alive and saying that she just wanted to know if he is up so he could keep her company on the phone while she drove home from work. He claimed she was just a friendly coworker, but I think that's inappropriate for a man in a relationship to constantly keep entertaining her and to only do it when his girlfriend was not around makes it even more suspicious. As the months went by, he continued talking to her for long periods of time many times throughout the week. He knew it bothered me, but he didn't care. One day I saw a text from her after he missed work one night and she was saying how he missed out on his burrito. It got to the point where the girl was even buying him food. One time he sent her a flirty text at 10:10 a.m. saying "You can run but you can't hide" It was obvious that he was interested in this girl and she was interested in him too. I ended up doing some research and finding out at the time this girl was only 24 years old and he was 39 years old. He just started working there in November 2019, he had only known her four months when they started talking, she's 15 years younger than him, always on the phone together and buying each other food.... but claimed that she was just a friend. One time he told me she was just "some nerd ass line lead bitch" I even contacted her a couple times because it got to the point where it was getting flat out disrespectful. She claimed she didn't know about me and that she wasn't interested in him in that way and that they were just work friends and would talk about work and food and his work frustrations and that she would stop contacting him. Then it stopped for a little bit but then started back up. Then I contacted her again and she said it's nothing going on and he's just her friend and she can't control when he answers his phone. So basically, she was going to keep calling as long as he allowed it. Which I thought was very embarrassing that my man was entertaining this young girl like this making her feel this comfortable with him and its even pathetic on her part because she knew about me at that point. It even got to the point where she felt comfortable enough to address me by my first name as if we were ever introduced. And she even mentioned before that he told her I don't like when he has female friends. That was not true because his actual best friend is a female and I never had any problem with her at all and whenever she came around and it was never any problem and he never had a problem talking to her on the phone around me. I'm very comfortable with his best friend. But he didn't do any of that with this coworker. On August 13, 2020 I took his phone out of my name and put it in his name. I was not about to keep paying his bill for him to keep entertaining her on my expense. Plus, that way will give him his full privacy and I won't be tempted to look when I suspect something. Anyway, when I did my research, I found out the girl's name and other little things about her and I noticed her birthday was coming soon. So, I made a mental note in my head "watch when her birthday comes around, something is going to happen" So that Friday September 4th, the day before her birthday I was right. Which was also the same day he agreed to watch our daughter but cancelled on me last minute because he had to work that night. When what it really was, was that he wanted to take this girl out for her birthday that morning, so he decided that was more important than watching our daughter so I wouldn't have to miss any work. Usually, he got off work at 6:30 a.m. and make it home around 7:45 a.m. and he would text me he made it home from work, and by that time I would be on my way to work and I would make it to work around 8:15 a.m. and call him and let him know I made it to work. That was our routine every morning. But that morning he never sent me a text letting me know he made it home, he never responded to my text and I called him three times and he didn't answer. I assumed he must have been taking her out to eat for her birthday. It was a Friday morning and he just got paid and he was ready to treat his new woman of interest out for her birthday. And I found out I was right. He randomly texted me that morning at 10:02 a.m. saying "made it" no explanation or anything, as if that is okay and I'm not concerned where he was. I'm sure if I got home from work at 8:30 p.m. instead of 6:10 p.m. and I didn't answer my phone during the time he knows I'm off and just came home as if that were normal, he would have a big problem with that. He still never once addressed this. Anytime it was something regarding the people at his job he would just up and leave and never say anything as if that's ok to do in a relationship and wonder why I be suspicious and think something going on. Anyway, on September 30, 2020 he ended up admitting that he took this girl who is now 25 years old, out to eat for her birthday. He still claimed it was nothing and that people at work buy each other food all the time, which is true I could understand that but why not just say that you are going out to eat with a coworker? Why not answer the phone or text back and just say that? Why come home as if nothing had happened? All that makes it even more suspicious. Also, on this same day September 30th, his phone had been off for about 2 weeks because he did not pay his phone bill so he could only text at the house on Wi-Fi or get facetime calls. So, when he would leave for work, he couldn't call or facetime and could only text if he were connected to Wi-Fi. I already knew about this old government phone he had that we would occasionally use to get on the party line. But I never saw it because he would always keep it hidden. So as his phone is off, he never once mentioned that he had this other phone with him in case he needed to make a call or something. He never even gave me the phone number to this phone. So, on September 19, 2020 he came home from work and his second phone was on the table. He wasn't expecting me to come down to turn on the monitor. I didn't say anything. Five minutes later I come down, it's gone of course. I still didn't say anything. I just thought it was strange that he never mentioned anything about carrying this phone and he sure didn't want me to see it. So of course, I assumed that he was using it to talk to her since his phone was off. So, on September 30, 2020 I ended up finding out that he was using the phone to talk to her after work and when he would get home, he would power the phone off. It's very strange that this young girl can have the phone number to that phone and his own girlfriend couldn't. This is another thing that confirmed my suspicion that there was something going on with this girl because there was even one day the week before where we said he thought he left the stove on downstairs but wasn't able to call me or text me so I could check. Which was not true at all because he had the other phone that he was using to talk to the girl, but he didn't want me to know that or know the number or that he had this phone with him, so he was willing to risk me and his daughter's life that day not knowing if he turned the stove off all because he didn't want me to know about this secret phone. Of course, he never saw any wrong in his actions. It got to the point where I felt like he was putting this woman before me and our child. It was disrespectful that he would keep entertaining her knowing I don't like it and knowing if it were me entertaining a male coworker the way he had been entertaining this girl then he would have a problem with it too and find it very suspicious. They started getting more and more comfortable with each other. He does not acknowledge my feelings or care how it made me feel. It was very embarrassing. He was unable to see things from my perspective and can't even understand why I feel the way I feel about this entire situation with this young girl. This is exactly how him and I got together. We were cool. I was 23 and he was 36 and we would talk on the phone a lot, like the way he started doing with her. Then we would buy each other food and go out to eat, like what he was doing with her. I saw the pattern. I knew there was something going on. All of this just wasn't a coincidence but of course he thought I was just overreacting and being insecure and crazy and he could never address any of those issues and was constantly disregarding my feelings so what was I supposed to think? I cried my eyes out to him about this and told him how much it hurt me, and he didn't care at all. I asked him what if I was doing all this with a male coworker and he felt the same way I felt? He said he would never find out because he would never invade my privacy and go through my phone. I can admit I was wrong for invading his privacy and going through his phone even when the phone was in my name. I can admit my wrongs. But that does not make this affair he was having with this coworker acceptable in any kind of way. He finally went on to say that if he saw I was communicating with a male coworker and taking him out to eat for his birthday and he thought it was something inappropriate going on, he would leave rather it was true or not. That was his way of saying if I don't like it then I can go, which he has said before many times whenever I try to talk to him about how he was hurting me. On October 7, 2020 all my suspicions were confirmed. I heard him on the phone with her. He didn't know I was listening. He was telling her I was crazy and telling her all these lies about me making it seem like I was a horrible person. He was basically trying to make it seem like I'm just his crazy baby mama that lived upstairs with his baby and he only come upstairs to see the baby. She was so comfortable. She was all winy and flirty and calling him bae and asking him about what he was eating and if he was going to come to work tonight and him calling her shorty and saying he was going to call her before he went to bed. Exactly how him and I used to talk. After that convo, I texted her and she was finally honest with me and let me know that yes she had a crush on him and liked him and that she didn't act on it because he had me but once he took her out for her birthday she really started to like him and said they actually started "talking" September 4th, but before that it was just a crush. She said at first she was trying not to be disrespectful towards me but I was doing things to her so she said why respect me when I wasn't respecting her, so she said she stopped holding back and that's when she really started to "like him like him" and that's when they began their actual relationship on September 4th the day he took her out for her birthday. I even found out that they did start actually having sex around this time and she was sending him money and he would lie about going to work certain nights so him and her could go spend nights at hotels with her. I even saw text messages that sometimes they would meet before work and she would give him oral sex. I saw all this coming back in March. A female knows when another female likes her man. I'm a female so I know how us females are when we like a man, we want to talk to him all the time and we do little things for them like buy them food and we just enjoy their company. I knew from the amount of time they spent on the phone together and the way she would text him wanting him to keep her company on the phone and her buying him food and from her text messages to me expressing how much of a good friend he is. It was obvious to me. He would leave for work earlier and earlier and would claim he was working all these days but then would also claim how broke he was because his paycheck didn't match his lies. She even ended her current relationship with the guy she was with because she felt like it was becoming something serious between them. He knowingly entertained this female that had a crush on him for months and had an affair with her, took her out and spent money on her, talked down on me to her, made her feel comfortable, cancelled on watching our daughter many times so he could take her out, was talking to her on secret phones I didn't even have the number to when his phone was off, downloaded text apps to talk to her and anytime I would bring up this female he would get mad and defensive and act like I was just insecure and crazy when in fact he was playing both of us. But of course, he blamed me for running him to the new supply. They never take responsibility for their actions. If they cheat it's because you made them. That is how they think, and it shows how messed up they are in the head. I understand people make mistakes. I made worse mistakes, but I can sincerely apologize and mean it and can see how I hurt the other person. Narcissist cannot do that. And after all of this came out and after I heard how horrible he talked about me to her, he just acted as if nothing happened. He did not want to talk about it and expected me to just forget all this. I could forgive the affair, but I could not keep forgiving someone who does not see a problem in their actions and can't take responsibility for any of their wrong doings and is constantly disregarding my feelings and disrespecting me. He would rather lose me as his girlfriend than to admit he was wrong. All of this is typical narcissist behavior. This is toxic and unhealthy. This is not love. Narcissist can turn love on and off because they use love as a manipulation tactic. I lost respect for him. That was the moment I really started emotionally detaching myself from him.

The love I had for him turned into pure disgust. The only good thing that came out of the relationship was our child. I felt so tricked and used. He's was not the guy he was in the beginning. He drained me. He took advantage of my kindness. He emotionally, verbally, and mentally abused me. He played me. I saw him for the monster her truly was. I really loved and cared about him. I would have done anything for him. He hurt me in so many ways and never once felt any remorse. I thought we would be a family and live happily ever after. I really thought he loved me and cared about me. I was fooled. I had to accept that none of this was real and that I was no different than any of the rest of his victims. I have even spoke with women that have been with him in the past and they all have very similar stories. But of course, to him we are all the crazy ones. Narcissist all follow a similar pattern.

The three stages of Narcissist Abuse are Idealize, Devalue, and Discard. This cycle will repeat if you allow it. The idealize stage is when they first get you and they are so sweet and caring and make you feel loved and they show you so much attention. Then after they know you're hooked; they start to devalue you. During this stage you can tell something is off, but you just can't figure out what it is. Their true colors start to show. They start to criticize everything about you. They constantly put you down and make it seem like it's the victim's fault. They also will try to devalue all the victim's friends, family, hobbies, etc. They will point out every small mistake you make and if you even nicely point out any mistake they make, they take it personal and become angry. The last stage is the discard stage. During the discard stage they treat you like you are nothing. You see them for the monster they truly are. They will disregard your feelings and treat you as if you don't deserve basic human decency. They act as if you are a bother to them. They do things and don't bother to explain it to you. Some days they pretend you are not there. It's obvious that something is wrong and if you mention their bizarre behavior to them, they say that you are crazy and making things up. They start distancing themselves and withdrawing from you and you have no idea why. This is the most brutal stage. By the time the victim makes it to this stage they are so emotionally damaged and confused. Be careful because they will try to love to bomb you and make you feel like they have changed but this is just another manipulation tactic and they will repeat the same three cycles.

Why stay with someone that treats you like this? Why not just leave?

It is so easy for someone who is not in the situation to say just leave and to say it could never be them. But it's not that simple. When you are in a relationship with a narcissist you become trauma bonded to them. According to psychology today, "Humans are wired to emotionally bond with the people around them. This ability to bond is the glue that keeps families and relationships together. When we feel endangered or insecure our natural reaction is to reach out to those we are bonded with for protection. But what happens when the person we are bonded to is the one who is mistreating us? Then our tendency to bond works against us. Under normal circumstances, we might be able to walk away from our abuser and look for help elsewhere. Unfortunately, the conditions that create trauma bonding are not at all normal. With "Narcissistic Trauma Bonding," you are initially showered with intense love and approval. It is like a fantasy come true. Then gradually the ratio of positive to negative events shifts—often so subtly that you cannot say exactly when this happened. You find yourself in fights with someone you desperately love who claims that everything bad that is happening is all your fault. Unless you walk out immediately and never look back, you are well on your way to becoming this person's psychic prisoner. You will find yourself "Trauma Bonded" to someone who is destroying you. This is like your own personal opiate addiction crisis. You are now addicted to this person's approval and only desire their love and no one else's. You know you should stop, but you do not have the willpower to do so on your own."

I had to really think about all the reasons I stayed and put up with that kind of abuse:

I wanted my daughter to grow up in the house with both her parents. In the beginning he was a good dad and loved her and I thought it would be cruel to just move away with her when we had been raising her together since she's been born. I think if we did not have a child together, I would have left him a long time ago. I understand that he could still be in her life even if we didn't live together but I wanted her to live with both of us and we both raise her together and for her to see us both every day and do the family thing. We had the whole house to ourselves. Our daughter and I stayed on the second floor and he stayed on the first floor and the only time he really came up was to see her or if I needed him to come upstairs and watch her for a few minutes. Other than that, when him and I would interact with each other when she was sleep or away, I would go downstairs, and we spend our time together or watch tv or something. But after a while it got to the point where I just stayed upstairs, and he stayed downstairs and came up whenever he wanted to see her. We both were still in the same house but on different floors and was able to raise our daughter together but still had our space away from each other. Plus, It was cheaper that way. Us splitting the monthly bills and the property tax twice a year was cheaper for both of us. It would cost way more money for both of us if we were living in two separate locations and trying to raise her. October 7, 2020 was when I finally ended the relationship. Even though to him whenever I would bring up how the things, he was doing was not appropriate for a man in a relationship he would angrily react "WHAT RELATIONSHIP??? THIS HAS NEVER BEEN A RELATIONSHIP" which was just another game narcissist play trying to get you to believe you are the problem and that they do no wrong and if they do it is because it's your fault. Anyway, this time I agreed with him. He was right, this was not a relationship. Once I accepted that, I started to feel relieved. I told him we could be cool for our daughter's sake and raise her and I wouldn't bother him unless it was regarding our daughter, the dog, a bill, something in the house, an emergency or something relevant. He agreed. I thought things would be perfect that way.....but when you are dealing with a narcissistic psychopath, it is never going to be easy.

But even after us ending the relationship and just co-parenting in the same house, he still found ways to give me a hard time and still tried to provoke negative reactions out of me which is typical narcissist behavior. Narcissist do not want peace or to resolve things. They love confusion and they love to play victim to scenarios they created. After ending the relationship on October 7, 2020, it was three situations that happened that let me know that co-parenting in the same house with him was not going to work out:

1. October 20, 2020: Since October 7th when I ended the relationship things were going great the first thirteen days but on October 20th he came home and didn't say anything to me and didn't even come up to see our daughter like he did every day when he came home from work. I instantly knew something was wrong so after a while I went downstairs and asked him was everything ok and I could tell something was wrong because as usual he started with the passive aggressive behavior "NOTHING IS WRONG" but clearly upset and when I asked him did he want to talk about it he said "I WILL NEVER TALK ABOUT IT" so it was clear that there was a problem and instead of talking about it like a normal person trying to resolve the issue he started acting like a child stomping around pouting with an attitude and then when you ask him about it he says nothing is wrong but clearly displaying that there is something wrong. I did not find out what he was about mad about until hours after I was checking my email and I saw that the day before I sent some gorilla shit to his coworker aka his side chick's house (this is legal to do from poopsenders.com) back on October 3rd and it did not get delivered until October 19th, so I had forgot all about it and I realized that's what he was mad about. This happened before October 7th when I ended the relationship so of course I was mad and disgusted with him and her because he was cheating on me with this woman and trying to make it seem like I was crazy. But after October 7th I honestly stopped caring about what he was doing. The delivery date was just after that point. I can understand why he would be mad and once I apologized to him and told him that was before I ended the relationship because since October 7th everything was cool. Of course, he couldn't see how I would be hurt because he was having sex with this woman and still having sex with me but it's typical for a narcissist to blame you for their cheating. A person that

is not toxic would also have communicated what they were mad about also in the beginning instead of coming home acting like a child and ignoring me and ignoring our child.

2. October 24, 2020: This day he came home and this particular morning he didn't come upstairs to see our daughter like he usually did so hours later he randomly comes upstairs and takes our daughter, puts her shoes on and started packing a bag with her diapers as if he was about to take her somewhere. He didn't say anything to me he just randomly came upstairs and took the baby and I asked him was he taking her to his sister house, and he said no then I asked him where he was taking her, and he ignored me and just proceeded to walk out and then I asked him again where he was taking her he got really mad at said "I DON'T HAVE TO TELL YOU SHIT RETARDTED BITCH" all of this came out of nowhere. It was so bizarre I could not believe it. We had not had an argument or anything. He just randomly came upstairs with an attitude and got offended when I asked him where he was taking our daughter. That's all I asked. What mother is going to let a man just come take her child with an attitude and pack her a bag and not ask where he is taking her? He did that to provoke a negative reaction out of me. That was completely uncalled for and very strange.

3. October 30, 2020: I asked him if he could watch the baby for a little while so I could run some errands. Not even an hour after I left he began facetiming me but my phone was in the car, so I wasn't able to answer it and I called him back when I got back to the car. He instantly got an attitude and hung up on me and when I called him back he did not answer so I knew right away he had an attitude because I did not answer his facetime. At that point we were not in a relationship anymore, we were just co-parenting. A few days before this day he acted like he was going to work and went and spent the night with the co worker and I never mentioned it because we weren't together and what he did was no longer my concern but me not answering his facetime and him wanting to know what I was doing was very delusional on his part. Narcissist can dish out all the disrespect and do what they want to do and don't like anyone to

question them but as soon as you give them a taste of their own medicine they can't handle it. The next day he didn't come up and see our daughter the entire day because he was mad at me for not answering his facetime and he was feeling so guilty about what he was doing with his coworker/side chick. He couldn't handle the same hurt he put me through. And I wasn't even trying to hurt him, I was simply doing me and minding my business not worried about him or what he was doing.

I'M FINALLY FREE

November 1, 2020 was the day I moved out. This was one of the best decisions I ever made in my life. The abuse was just getting worse and I knew it was not going to get any better. As bad as I wanted my daughter to grow up in the same house with both parents, sometimes things just do not work out the way we want them too. I had to accept that. I also had to think about what was best for my daughter. I did not want her to think it is okay to allow a man to treat her like this. I did not want her to think any of this was okay. Being a single parent is better than letting your child see you in a toxic abusive relationship. When I moved out I felt so free. I had my life back. When I moved out things instantly got better. I started receiving so many different blessings. Since I was narc free I was able to do little things that I was not able to do when I was with him. I was able to go shopping, I was able to cook, I was able to save money, I was able to go out and get some air without anybody criticizing me or accusing me of doing stuff I was not doing. I was able to go see family and friends without having to prove what I was doing every second I was gone. I did not have to worry about anyone trying to control or manipulate me anymore. The three years I was with him I was not able to do a lot of things because I was afraid of how he would react or what he would think. I did not have to worry about any of that anymore. God is so good!

The only feeling I have for him is pure disgust. I don't miss him. There are some people that miss their narc when they leave them, but I didn't miss any of his abuse. It was nothing to miss. The person he was in the beginning was not who he truly was. I saw him for the pathetic individual he truly was. The love I had for him died way before I moved out. I wish I would have known what he was in the beginning. He started denying our daughter only because I moved out and moved on with my life. When he was sneaking around with the coworker and I was home crying and taking care of our daughter it was okay but as soon as I began to move on with my life and not sit around and continue to let him hurt me, then he decides not to have anything to do with our daughter anymore. It's the nerve and the audacity that really gets me. Overall, he is the true definition of a bum and sorry excuse for a man. I was there for him when he was at his lowest. I put him before myself. I tried my best to make sure he was happy. I showered him with gifts, love, money, etc. When I think about how much of pathetic loser he is, it makes me sick to my stomach. All he did was use me and take advantage of me. Before our daughter was born he had not had a job in years. I pressed him to get a job so he could help with our daughter because I was tired of supporting all of us alone. He lives off women. He spends all his money on cigarettes, weed and liquor. He was very irresponsible. He never saved money. He had the mindset of a child. He was not attractive at all. The sex was not the best. His communication skills sucked. He thought he was 20 years younger than what he actually was. He was always broke and he felt everything in life should be handed to him. His bills were never paid on time. He didn't care about running a bill up until he got a disconnection notice.

Its normal for victims to never want to get in a relationship again after being with a narcissist. I think that me being a misanthropist already and before I even got in this relationship, I didn't think relationships was something I would be interested in because I already had trust issues with humans and being around humans and dealing with them is an unpleasant experience for me. After this horrible experience, I know now I should have stuck with my original thought. This experience changed me forever. If I were able to have my same exact child with another man I would but since that is not possible I have to accept the situation for what it is. My daughter is one of the best things that happened to me but the relationship with her dad was one of the worse experiences I have ever went through in my life. But I know I would never have had my daughter if the relationship with her dad never started so I take it as a life lesson. Relationships are not for everybody. I understand that one bad relationship should not make you want to give up on dating, but my situation is different. I know myself and I know what I want, and I know what I do not need. My main goals are raising and taking care of my daughter, finishing school, expanding my business, healing, and becoming a better me. I do not have any time for a relationship. I am not saying that I will never get in a relationship again because we never know what God has for us in the future. But right now, it is not what I want and would be a distraction to what I am trying to work towards in my life.

I emotionally detached myself from him back in October once I confirmed all my suspicion about his co-worker was true. Me staying in the same house with him for the rest of October was because I really wanted my daughter in the house with both of her parents. But once he noticed that I was truly over the relationship and he could no longer control me and that my attention was elsewhere that is when he also started to take his anger out on our daughter. He stopped coming upstairs to see her, stop liking her pictures I sent him of her and the day I moved out he even sat her car seat outside where they pick up the garbage and put a garbage bag on it. The day I moved out I asked him would he still be in her life and he said yes. That is all I wanted. But he did the exact opposite. When he threw her car seat out to the garbage he already had the intention of not being in her life anymore. Only because I asked him would he still be in her life. Our relationship was over, but I still wanted my daughter to have her dad in her life. He knew how strong

I felt about my daughter having her dad in her life. I was a daddy's girl, and my dad was my world, and I was his baby till the day he died. My dad died right after I turned 24 years old and that broke my heart. My dad was in my life the entire 24 years, we talked every day and he spoiled me even when I was an adult. We were inseparable. I wanted my daughter to have the same father daughter relationship with her dad like I had with my dad. He knew that he no longer had control over me and that I have moved on from the relationship and I had him all figured out (Narcs hate when you have them figured out) so he did the only thing he thought could possibly hurt me and that was to start denying our daughter. He became a true dead beat. Even though this is typical for narcissist to do, I can honestly say this surprised me about him because I know he loves his children. The day I moved out was the last time he saw our daughter and never checked on her again after that. No calls, no texts, did not send money for diapers or milk or anything. He changed his number, so I did not have his number to contact him, but he had my number. The only time I heard him was when he would get on the party line (the chatline we met on) and when he would get on there I never spoke to him but I would hear him and all he did was bash me and say our child was not his and that he was only helping me with the child because we were together and its always "mama's baby, papa's maybe" and how he never took a blood test and he'll see the child in 18 years and we'll see if she really is his. All of this is on recording in case he ever tried to deny saying any of this. All of this was a shock to me because I never once thought he would deny his child and I know he loved her, but narcs will do anything they can to hurt you especially if you finally get the strength to leave them. I know he wanted to hurt me by denying our child, but he does not even realize the only person he is really hurting is his daughter. When people on the party line would ask him about the baby he would say he only had two daughters instead of three. Somebody asked him would he still see the baby and his exact response was "Tell that bitch to put a picture of the baby on the party line page and yall send it to me and I'll see the lil muthafucka" another time I was on the party line and somebody connected him in the room and my daughter was in the background and somebody asked why they connected the rooms and he screamed out "SO WE COULD HEAR THIS BITCH AND HER BABY" he was clearly trying to get a reaction out of me but I ignored it. I never thought I would hear him say such horrible things about his own child and just deny her like that. I know it's all to hurt me but after hearing some of the outrageous things he said about her it made me think what if one day he does reach out to me to see his child, how do I know he won't do something to her just to hurt me? It is very common for a narcissist to use their child to hurt the other parent. He also said that if I put him on child support he would quit his job and I wouldn't get anything and if I did it wouldn't be much anyway. He would also brag about buying half's of weed, liquor and new shoes during this time instead of sending money to help support his child. He also mentioned one day that now he can put away $50 a week for a new watch since he didn't have to buy diapers anymore…..but he only bought diapers for her 4 times and then there was one time he gave me half on her diapers in the 18 months that he was in her life so him saying he bought diapers was just trying to make it seem like he was doing his part financially when he really wasn't. In the beginning when she was born he was a great dad, not financially but as far as being there. He would give her baths, watch her while I was at work, cook for her, get her dressed, etc. But as time went on things changed. As him and his coworker got closer he decided that he could not watch our daughter anymore on certain days because he worked nights. I worked during the day, was in school full time and still had to come home and be a mother. I could not just make excuses not to be a mom. He was only a father to our daughter when it was convenient for him or when him and I were on good terms. It was more important to him to hang out and lollygag around after work with the coworker instead of coming home right after work to watch the baby so I could leave for work. My mom was helping me a lot with watching the baby but she also had other stuff going on in her life so I couldn't keep burdening her and I know she was helping me as much as she could and even my sister was helping too and his sister was also helping a lot at first so I just needed him to watch her for two days a week and when I explained this to him he got really defensive about it and eventually I got really stressed and had my own other issues I was dealing with. I really loved my job and loved what I was doing and loved my boss, but I got really stressed out, he wouldn't compromise and watch her during the day for me anymore even though she is both our responsibility plus other issues I was having with my job so I made the decision to quit my job so I could stay home with our daughter and said I would just have to get a work from home job. Once you see a narcissist for who they truly are and the mask comes off, you will see how pathetic they are. Like I said before I already emotionally detached myself from him in October so all the love I had for him was already dead before I moved out the house. I became really disgusted with him. He even bragged about how he had raw sex with the coworker in September while him and I were still together and the last day him and I had sex was October 4th, so he risked my life, not knowing if she had any std's or any other diseases and it was also during the pandemic. Not saying that I never cheated but I cheated on him in the beginning of our relationship and during my pregnancy but once our child was born I never cheated on him or messed with anyone else until after I ended the relationship. The encounters I had at the beginning of our relationship and while I was pregnant was all protected. Not saying that makes it any better but I was able to admit my wrongs and feel bad for what I did. This is something narcissist cannot do. Soon after I moved out he began disrespecting his new girlfriend by going on the party line and talking to a few of his Ex's and the one he was with before me he even tried to invite her over and spent hours on the party line flirting with her. He even mentioned that after I moved out his new girlfriend came the same day and brought him a bigger tv and microwave and he started talking about how he can get money out of her anytime he wanted and how she wanted to buy him a truck and they go half on the payments and how he can basically get anything he wanted out of her. She's a year younger than I am. He tricked her the same way he did me. He's going to use her and financially abuse her and take advantage of her just like he did me. The narcissist doesn't really care about you, they only care what you can do for them. The same things he told her about me is the same thing he told me about the lady he was with before me.

"Psychopaths keep their exes strung along for added attention and triangulation. They use exes to appear in high demand at all times, creating competition and jealousy with their current partners. Their exes can usually be places into two categories: 1. In love with me 2. Crazy" -Psychopath free by Jackson MacKenzie

"Narcissists are masters of illusion, they play the poor abused victim while in truth they are wreaking havoc by torturing, mistreating and abusing those that they fooled into loving them" – Y.Clerebout

"They will purposely get you to react by probing and prodding and doing things they know will upset you or set you off. They will treat you with such a lack of respect that you have a hard time holding back and then you explode. Screaming and acting crazy and saying awful things back to them. Appearing like you are the out of control one. Don't fall for it, don't react, respond. Either walk away or calmly respond. They want you to react in a out of control manner so they can point the finger at you and say, "She/he is crazy." -–– Maria Consiglio @understandingthenarc

SMEAR CAMPAIGN

The smear campaign started way before I moved out but got even worse when I finally did move out. When a narcissist cannot control you anymore and you leave them they will to tell everyone they know how horrible you are and how much of a victim they are and that are you really the crazy abusive one. When they no longer can control you, they will try to control the way everyone else sees you. This is very typical for narcissist to do. He started telling people I was crazy and demonic and that I needed help. He would never tell what he did to me, he would only describe my reactions. He made it seem like I was picking on his new girlfriend, the same coworker that he claimed was just a friend which ended up being his side chick and then his new girlfriend when I left him. He claimed I was just insecure when I was really on point. He made it seem like I am the reason he does not see his child anymore when he never contacted me about seeing her after I moved out and instantly started denying her. The only reason I stayed in that miserable situation that long is because I wanted him in her life. Even after we ended the relationship I tried to be cool with him so we could co parent. He bashed me to anyone that would listen to make it seem like he was the victim in the situation. Way after I moved out he started telling people I was mad because I still wanted him which was the furthest from the truth. He knew he lost me. Once I emotionally detached myself from him I never felt the same way about him again because I saw his true colors and accepted what he really was. When our daughter was born I never messed with another man until after I ended the relationship. I wanted to keep our family together. Even though I knew he had been having an affair with the co worker for months, I thought maybe he would realize what he had. But after the constant heartbreak and disappointment the love I had for him finally died. Once I moved on from him sexually to someone else I knew I was over him. There was nothing left. I had already been feeling unloved and unappreciated. I was totally turned off from him. Everything about him from the way he would treat me, how he talked to me, how he took advantage of me, how he would treat our daughter when he was mad at me disgusted me. But of course, he wanted everyone to believe that I was just crazy and still in love with him and still wanted him and I was losing it and doing all these horrible things to him. They want to make themselves look good and want to make it seem like you are the abuser. The best thing to do is ignore it. They want you to respond in a crazy negative way so they can make it seem like it is really you. They all do this. Do not fall for it.

"Relationships with Narcissists always end badly, so be prepared for the inevitable. They will turn others against you, they will try to ruin your reputation, they will continue to deny everything, and of course they will blame you." -unknown (took from Instagram page @life_afterawakening)

FLYING MONKEYS

Narcissist do not abuse everyone they encounter so it very discouraging to victims when people would disregard the victim's feelings when it comes to the abuser. To the outside world, the narcissist might seem cool and calm but in the home the narcissist is one of the evilest heartless creatures you will ever meet. They are very good at playing the victim and getting other people to believe that they are innocent, and you are the evil one. Narcissist have flying monkeys; those are people who side with the narcissist no matter what. In their eyes the narcissist can do no wrong. This is the person that will believe all the bad things the narcissist says about you without even hearing your side of the story. In this case, his flying monkey was his sister. She did not think her brother could do any wrong. She believed all the negative things he told her about me but whenever I would try to tell my side she would say she didn't want to be involved or she didn't want to hear those things about her brother but then on the other hand when her brother would tell her things I did to him she would text me asking why I did that or telling me to leave him alone because he's not bothering me and basically trying to make it seem like I was the abuser when in reality all of my actions were a response to his abuse. She would tell me things like "I know my brother loves you because he told me he never cheated on you" which was the same thing she told the female he was with before me. None of it was real. She was his flying monkey and she tried to act like he was God's gift to women, and he was the perfect spouse, and this was all far from the truth. She was one of the few that he really had fooled because some of his other friends and family knew exactly what I was talking about when I would describe this kind of abuse because they knew him and how he could get at times. Even though I saw the worse of him. After I left him for good he told everyone about all the things I did to him but left out what he did to me.

"Flying monkeys are the enablers who support the narcissist no matter what. The flying monkeys blindly side, encourage, support, and even abuse the victim, to defend the narcissist. Even if they know the narcissist is wrong or doing very bad things. They are either blind to the narcissist's behaviors because of cognitive dissonance, or they just don't care. Either way they are just as guilty. Narcissists usually have a few flying monkeys that they count on for back up." — Maria Consiglio @understandingthenarc

THE PARTY LINE

You can be anything you want to be on the party line. He has been calling the party line for over 20 years, so the party line has been a big part of his life. Most of the women that he has been in a relationship with or had sex with, he met from the party line. All the women he has children with he also met from the party line. When he is on the party line he tells people that he is a "Don" and brags about money he does not have and brags about having sex with all these different women. He has had sex with a lot of women from the party line but that is because he does not have a standard when it comes to women. He will have sex with any woman that gives him the time of day. He does not care what race, what size, what age, what mental state, etc. Majority of the women that he had sex with on the party line are overweight, not attractive or have some kind of disability. No disrespect to the women that he has messed with but that is to make a point that the only reason his party line body count is so high is because he will have sex with any woman that shows him interest. There have been maybe 3 attractive women in my opinion that he messed with from the party line (going off the ones I saw). He is known on the party line for using and abusing women. He uses women for their money and to buy him things and he also gets abusive with them rather it be physically, mentally, emotionally, or verbally. He gets tough and abusive with women because he knows as big as he is he can easily overpower them. Whenever he would get into arguments with men on the party line it would never end good for him. One time he got into an argument with a guy on the party line and the guy pulled out a gun on him and he got really scared and told the guy "We better than this. You really about to let the party line make us fight" another time he went to a party line party and he got disrespectful with a transexual male and called him a homophobic slur and the transexual male knocked him unconscious. There was another time when he went to the movies with a known gay male on the party line and some of the other men on the party line gave him a hard time about that and made jokes about him and he got defensive and would argue with a lot of the men on there and gave out his address, but he never actually had a real physical fight with a man. He took out all his anger on the women he was dealing with. One time one of the females he was messing with got slapped in the mouth by another man from the party line and instead of him defending her he told her "you shouldn't have been running your mouth so much" he did not dare say anything to the man. He was very controlling and there were times when he found out about one of the females he was messing with talked with another man or had sex with another man and he would get abusive with the females and down talk the men to the females but then turn around and act like he was cool with the men to their face or over the phone. Along time ago he got a settlement check for $250,000 and he ran through that money so fast and was right back broke. But when he had that money that is when a lot of the females on the party line wanted to meet with him and mess with him. He used that money to attract women and the same guy that pulled the gun out on him he ended up buying him a car. Since the party line is over the phone you can talk to people before you meet them and that gave him an advantage. He said before that he didn't send out pictures of himself or send out pictures of his private part because he "didn't want to ruin the element of surprise" and that was because his physical appearance is not attractive at all and his private area is not what you would expect it to be so he talks to women over the phone and pretends to be charming, and his outgoing funny personality is what attracts the women so they fall in love with his phone personality before they meet him and when they actually do meet him they look past his looks and his sex and they start to fall in love with him just off his personality but when you really get to know him and the mask comes off you find out that he is not the person you thought he was and see him for the monster he truly is. On the party line he is this cocky loud outgoing guy that claimed to have guns, robs people, smokes the best weed and liquor, has all the women, etc. But in person he is a sensitive, childish, abusive, broke, hypocritical, irresponsible, insecure, sorry excuse for a man. He claims that he has never been physically abusive to a woman but that's the furthest from the truth. He admitted to me before that he slapped one woman while he had a ring on and left a mark under her eye and even spit on her. In the 3 years and 4 months I was with him he got physically abusive with me 3 times. It has also been confirmed that he was abusive to a few other women that he met from the party line. When his relationships with the women would end he would get back on the party line and bash and sneak diss the woman and blame the woman for the reason the relationship ended.

NON-FICTIONAL STORIES FROM HELL (NOT IN CHRONOLOGICAL ORDER)

The rest of this book will be me talking about different scenarios that happened throughout the relationship (June 2017 – October 2020).

The coworker situation and everything that happened with that situation leading up till October 7, 2020 was just the last straw. The abuse started way before then.......

- When I was pregnant with our daughter, I was paying him rent to live in the house. At the time he was not working (He was not working when we first got together and he did not get his job until November 2019, about 7 months after our child was born). After I had our baby, I was only off work for 3 weeks (I didn't think that was enough time) because he would not give me a break on rent that month so I had to go back to work after just having OUR baby so I could pay him rent. And the money I was paying him for rent at the time was not going to any household bills because they were not a priority to him. The money I was paying him for rent was to support his cigarette, liquor and weed habit.

- One time a girl he used to mess with before me just randomly came and pulled up to this house. We were all outside. She did not see me sitting in the car nor did she know him, and I were together. As she pulls up, she's yelling out the window at him "Hey [his name] I miss you. Take my number down" He took her number down right in front of me and gave her a cup of what he was drinking. Two of his friends were even right there to witness it. The entire situation was just flat out disrespectful. Because I'm sure if a guy I used to mess with just randomly popped up at the house saying he missed me and wanted me to take his number down and I did then it would have been a big problem.

- One year for his birthday I bought him two bottles of Hennessey for his birthday and instead of being grateful he gets mad and says "Why wouldn't you just give me money? I told you just get me money. I already know everybody else is going to buy me liquor, so I was going to have liquor" (or something in that context). I had already paid him rent for that month, had my own bills to pay plus was trying to save money. The two bottles of Hennessey I bought him I paid with on my credit card. He was so mad and ungrateful the next day I ended up going to the ATM and giving him a card with $100 in it just so he would not be mad. The next month for my birthday he bought me a $3 card and about $8 worth of snacks on his link card. I did not complain nor was I ungrateful. I did not try and make him feel bad about his gift like he did mines the month before.

- The taxes on his house had not been paid in years and the taxes was sold and the sheriff served him papers stating that if he did not pay the cost of redemption, he would lose the house. So, I went downtown and got the cost of redemption which was $10,249.21. I took out a $10,000 loan to pay it making my credit score go down so he would not lose his childhood home, the same home he bought for his mom before she died. When he called his friends and family members and told them the amount of redemption, none of them were able to help him at the time. But I made sure he did not lose that house because me, him and our daughter was living there, and I wanted to keep the family together. A normal person would be very grateful and appreciative that I saved the house but instead he acted as if that were something I was supposed to do because we were together. Before I did that he was charging me rent to stay in the house. After I did that I told him it would be best that instead of me paying him rent we would just split the monthly cost of the loans anI would put all the bills in my name, and we would split everything half and half. Before that he had the bills in his name and other people's names and he was not paying anything, everything was overdue. But once I put everything in my name, I made sure everything was paid and kept up with due dates and would remind him days before when each bill is due so he could give me his half. Every time he would give me his half for a bill he would tell people I was taking all his money. He felt that he should not have to pay any bills if he had a woman around. He mentioned before "All my bitches take care of me. I don't mess with bitches that can't do shit for me." He's so used to people babying him and taking care of his responsibilities for him that he doesn't know how to be a real man and handle his responsibilities so me asking him for his half of a bill was disrespectful to him.

- One time I bought him a Nike short outfit and a belt. He seemed happy but then he noticed I had on a new shirt. It was a $25 shirt that had the street I grew up on. Soon as he saw my shirt he said "YOU A SNAKE…. WHY YOU AINT BUY ME A SHIRT" I got his Nike outfit and his belt that same exact day which costed way more than my $25 shirt. This happened a lot in the relationship. I was only able to buy things if I get him the same thing. If I bought something for myself then it would become a problem or argument, or he would say things to try and make me feel bad for spending my money on myself. In the three years we were together I only went shopping one time for myself and that was because after I had the baby I was not able to fit any of my clothes and needed some new work clothes so I went to DD's discount and spent $300 and got me a bunch of some pants and shirts and hoodies I could fit. This was all my money. But as soon as I got back he said "U SPENT $300 AND DIDN'T BUY ME ANYTHING" even though I was always giving him money and buying him gifts and supporting his habit. It was okay for him to go out and spend his money on what he wanted to spend it on, and I never expected anything because we each had our own money, but I wasn't allowed to shop, treat myself or do anything unless I made sure I got him the same thing or more.

- He would always bring up how I invaded his privacy and went through his phone which I admit was wrong. But he also invaded my privacy. I didn't get much mail to the house because most of my mail went to my P.O. box but when I would get mail he would always open my mail and would never give it to me, and I thought that was very strange. I found out from the covert narcissist support group I am in on Facebook that this is common for narcissist to do. I remember one day he said the sheriff sent a letter to everyone in the house and they sent me one too and when I asked him where it was he said he had to find it. Another time I got a letter from the post office about informed delivery and I saw it opened sitting on his table. He never said anything about it. One time I ordered a thermometer and he opened it as if it were his and was like "Your thermometer came" and I did not say anything because I did not want to start an argument, but this was a big invasion of privacy. I also know I invaded his privacy by going through his phone a couple times, so I did not want to make a big deal out of it because we both invaded each other's privacy. The difference is, I can admit I was wrong, but he could never acknowledge any of his wrongs. In the entire three years and four months that we were together, he only apologized to me two times.

- One time our daughter spent the night at my sister house. There was a girl that I used to go to school with who mom makes and sells drunk uno game kits and she lived in the same town as my sister so the next day after work when I was going to get our daughter from my sister house I messaged the girl, and she gave me the address and I bought the game from her. I did not get out the car or anything, it was a simple exchange, when I texted and told her I was outside, she told her sister to bring it down, I gave her the $25 and drove off. That was it. Less than two minutes. Nothing else to the story. About ten minutes after I made it to my sister house. So, when I got to my sister house to pick up my daughter, my niece started crying because she did not want my daughter to leave and wanted her to stay another night. So, I said yes, and I went back home (at this time him and I wasn't staying together). I let him know that she was staying the night at my sister house again and later when I got in I showed him a picture of the uno game because I was excited and him and I were just recently talking about it. He instantly got an attitude and asked how I got the uno game. I told him a girl I went to school with mom makes them and sells them and she lives in the same town as my sister. He instantly got mad saying it does not make any sense that I went to get my daughter and came home without her and now suddenly I randomly got an uno game that I never told him about. He then gave me the silent treatment and later expressed that my story made no sense and how much of a liar I am and that I should have told him about the uno game. Me buying a simple uno game was a problem for him because I did not tell him about it. Even though I instantly showed him a picture of it as soon as I got in. He felt that I was supposed to let him know before I bought the game. Narcissists get mad at little things like this all the time. They are very controlling and feel like they need to know your every move, what you are doing with YOUR money, etc. They are very insecure and suspicious of everything you do because they know the things they do. But when it's the other way around they don't feel the need to tell you anything and can do as they please and you better not dare question them.

- Narcissist feel entitled to everything you have, especially your money. They are very financially dependent. One time his friend told me about this program and only certain people qualified. I qualified but he did not. I heard about the program before from other people I knew but I did not think it was legit until I heard about it from his friend and she confirmed it was legit. So, I applied and the money I got from it he felt like was supposed to be his even though it had nothing to do with him and everything was in my name. I used the money to pay off the two loans I took out for saving his house, I paid off some other bills, paid for my schoolbooks that semester and some other stuff. I used the money in a responsible way. Instead of me doing that he excepted me to give him most of the money so he could buy cigarettes, weed, alcohol, fake belts, and shoes. From what was left I gave him $500 out of it and his response was "Thank you for the $500. Enjoy the rest of all your money" which was his way of showing how ungrateful and irresponsible he was. I put priorities first before fun. Something he could never do. After I gave him the $500 he gave me the silent treatment for the rest of the day because he felt I should have given him more money. I did not have to give him anything and if I would have known he was going to act like that anyway I would have kept the $500 and did something productive with it. He felt like I should have only paid off one of the loans I took out to save the house instead of both of them. Narcissists are very ungrateful and regardless to how much you do for them and give them nothing will ever be enough.

- If he wanted sex and I was too tired or was not in the mood then he would get an attitude and give me the silent treatment and start acting very passive aggressive. But if I wanted sex and he was not in the mood or too tired he would just brush me off and I would have to accept it. In the beginning of our relationship, I was the only one working and sometimes I would be tired, and he did not understand that but when he finally got a job and started working and he was working nights and on his feet all the time I understood that he was tired sometimes plus we had a baby also, so I was able to understand all those things. In the beginning when he was not working and we did not have a baby, he did not care about what I had going on. When we first started our relationship, I did not enjoy the sex at all. It was not what I liked nor what I was used too. But I liked him, and I loved the person who he pretended to be, so I dealt with the bad sex. But as time went on I grew to like it and I made the best out of what I had. And unlike the other men that I messed with before, this relationship was more than just sex, so I was able to look pass the sex and I loved him for him. But there were a couple times when it was good. Sex always had to be his way. It was very rare that we did the things I wanted to do when it came to sex. He expected oral sex almost every time we had sex but did not feel like he should give it in return. Even though that is something I do not really care for. One time I had not gave him oral sex in about a month and he got mad and said I must be giving it to someone else but when he said this, it was also over a year since the last time he gave me oral sex. In our three years and 4 months we were together, I gave him oral sex 526 times and only received it 17 times from him. This is just another example of how narcissist only care about their needs and do not really care about yours.

- Another thing that is very typical for narcissist to do is to just up and leave for hours without saying anything and come back like nothing ever happened. This happened quite often. In their mind this is okay for them to do but if you do it then all hell will break loose. One day he went to a party with some of his coworkers and instead of just saying he was going he just up and left and did not say anything and did not answer his phone. He was gone the entire night and did not come home until like 2 a.m. and his excuse for not just saying he was going to the party was because he knew I would get mad. I was mad because he just upped and left me home with the baby and not said anything and thinking I would not be worried. I do not care about him going to a party but I'm sure if I just up and left and went to a party for hours and left him home with the baby and then came home hours later and didn't answer my phone the entire time I was gone, he would have a problem with it also. Behavior like this is very typical for Narcissists. They never see the wrong in their actions but if you dare behave like them or give them a taste of their own medicine then you will never hear the end of it.

- During the COVID-19 pandemic when they were giving people stimulus checks. He knew he was not getting one because he owed child support. So, he kept asking me was I getting one and how much I was going to give him and started talking about all these different things he could do with the money. The day stimulus checks were deposited for most people, he was at work and I assume one of his coworkers let him know they got theirs, so he started texting me from work "Did you get your stimulus check?" and he already knew I was getting one and at first I told him no because I actually had bills and other things I needed to use the money for but of course he felt entitled and if I didn't give him anything then he would start treating me and the baby horrible so I kept the $1200 and gave him the $500 portion they sent for the baby and just like always he used the money to support his cigarette, weed, and liquor habit. He did not use the money to get new tires for his car like he said he would. We were both working but he was making more per hour than I was. A few months later he received a letter in the mail saying people who did not receive a stimulus check could fill out and still get it and he filled it out and because he owed child support they took a portion of it and sent him the rest and when he got his he paraded it around and was so excited and didn't think to give me any of his even though by that time I already had to quit my job because he wouldn't help me watch our daughter anymore while I work, I was still buying all the baby stuff she needed like diapers and wipes. He helped buy her milk 4 times on his link card so I will him credit for that. And one time even though he argued with me about it at first he finally gave me

$20 on a box of her diapers I bought. But at this time, I had my savings account and some other money coming in and he was working full time, but I still was the one making sure our daughter had all she needed, and I still always kept up my half of the bills and sometimes he wouldn't even have his half and I would gone head and pay the entire thing and let him pay me back later because the bills were in my name and I didn't want any late marks. He was very irresponsible with money. And when I brought up how I gave him a portion of my stimulus check and he did not give me any part of his, his response was "I FED YOU. I JUST BOUGHT U SOME FOOD THE OTHER DAY" I didn't argue with him because he never sees anything wrong with his actions so that would have just been a waste of time. It was the principle about it.

- One day at work I saw that Chuck E. Cheese had the $5 pizzas and $5 wings so for lunch I decided to go to Chuck E. Cheese and get a pizza and wings and while I was there waiting for the food, the person that worked at Chuck E. Cheese asked everybody if they had kids and all the people that had kids they gave them a stack of tickets for the wait. So, I took the tickets home and when I showed him the tickets they gave me for the baby his response was "I DIDN'T KNOW ANYTHING ABOUT YOU GOING TO CHUCK E. CHEESE" even though I only went there to get some lunch and it was less than five minutes away from my job. I sent him a picture of my lunch that same day, so I did let him know that is where I was going to get lunch, he just did not remember or was either sleep when I sent it to him Anytime I would mention any kind of small detail in my life like some food I ate or somewhere I went he would get defensive and say "I DIDN'T KNOW ANYTHING ABOUT THAT". Simple things like this were always a problem. I tried to always let him know every single place I went so there was not any problems later and sometimes he would swear I never told him and thought I was out being sneaky doing something I was not supposed to do. But when it comes to him he never gave me the same kind of respect. Narcissists hold you to certain standards and expect you to follow certain rules they do not follow themselves.

- During my pregnancy I started filling out job applications for him so he could get a job before our child was born and he would be able to bring some money into the house. He had not had a job in years except for selling weed. I was filling out so many applications for him while I was pregnant and even while I was at work. I worked my entire pregnancy until two days before our child was born because I was supporting me and him and he was still charging me rent to live in the house. All the places I was applying to for him he always had a complaint about. Most of them he missed interviews or would not call back because he said he would never work that kind of job. He was okay with letting his 9-month pregnant girlfriend work and pay rent and stress about not having any other help financially with the baby. So, when the baby was born, and I was working at the beginning he would watch the baby and take care our her while I was at work and I really appreciated that, but I wanted him to get a job to help financially. One day he brought up his other baby mama and said "I bet [her name] make sure her man taken care of. I bet he got on the new shoes. He don't work but I bet he makes sure the kids and house straight" I could not believe he said that because I was doing as much as I could for him. I was paying him $400 a month rent, I was constantly showering him with gifts and doing a lot for him but nothing I did was ever enough. One day I was honest and told him I was not about to keep supporting and taking care of a grown man. It was too much for me and his expectations were not realistic. He got defensive and of course gave me the silent treatment and went outside and started bashing me to his friends. Nothing I said was untrue. I did not mind giving him gifts every now and then and but should be something I did on my own, not something I was required to do. He was not working or even selling weed anymore. He felt because he was staying at home with our child then I should have been buying him shoes and clothes and giving him money besides the $400 a month rent I was giving him. I do not see how he thought I should pay him and buy him things for being a father to his own child. He was home all day anyway, the least he could do was watch the baby while I worked.

- The first time I moved out we were still in a relationship; I was pregnant, and we were still talking everyday but one day he was on the party line while I was at work and the lady he was in a relationship with before me was on there also and he begged her for hours to bring him some cigarettes. He had a car and had his own money for the cigarettes, but he wanted her to bring him some cigarettes. She finally gave in and went and bought the cigarettes and dropped them off to him and he gave her the money for his cigarettes and money for hers. The entire situation was disrespectful because he never mentioned it to me, I had to hear about it on the party line. At first he lied about it and said it did not happen then a few months later he admitted that he wanted to have sex with her, and he really did not need her to go get cigarettes. He said he could have gone and got the cigarettes himself and he just wanted to get her over there and I should be telling her thank you because if she would have wanted to come in he would have let her and had sex with her and would have just apologized to me later. I asked him what if I had a dude I mess with come drop me off a bottle of Hennessey, how would he feel? He said, "Do it and see what happens" Eventually he apologized. In the entire relationship he only apologized to me two times.

- One day he was going to Walmart and said he needed to get some deodorant and soap and body wash. I needed some deodorant also and some summers eve so I asked him could he get me some secret deodorant and some summers eve, and I would give him the money. He instantly said "HELL NAW IM NOT WALKING AROUND WITH THAT SHIT IN MY CART" I was so confused because there have been plenty of times when I went to the store and I got his body wash, soap, deodorant, and other things he needs. I even facetime him when I was there so he can make sure I was getting the right thing. Majority of the time I would buy his stuff and not even ask him for the money but there would be sometimes he would give me the money for it. But the one time I ask him to get my stuff it was a problem and I even told him I would give him the money for it. He eventually said he would get my deodorant, but he would not get the summers eve. He said as a man that is something he would not do. I understand some men might not want to get feminine products at the store but there are a lot of men that buy their woman's feminine products for them especially if they are already going to the store. But I did not press the issue. He went to the store and got all his stuff and did not even get my deodorant like he said he would. He claimed he forgot. So, I had to go all the way to the store and make a separate trip and get my own deodorant and summers eve. This is typical narcissist behavior. They will often "forget" things you need but remember all of theirs. If I would have went to the store and got everything I needed and just ignored all the stuff he needed it would have been a big problem when I got home.

- Even though we lived in the same house and both of us were equally responsible for our daughter, there were plenty of times when I felt our roles were not equal as parents. Regardless to what I had going on in my life or what I wanted to do, I had to be a mother first. I could not just leave out or spend my money on non-sense and automatically assume the other parent would handle it. Sometimes he would be a great dad and other times it would depend on the situation. Sometimes if he were really mad at me he wouldn't come upstairs to see the baby. He was able to do whatever he wanted or go wherever he wanted because he always assumed that I would be the one to stay in the house with the baby. When there were things I needed to do or had somewhere to go, I had to ask him to watch her and sometimes he would if I had to go to the store or make a quick run but if it took longer than an hour he would be calling me while I was out or facetiming me making me feel rushed. I never had any me time. The only real break I would have was when my mom or sister would keep the baby a night for me. When it came to buying stuff, she needed I could not just "see what I could do" I could not be a sometime parent. One time he even said to me that I was the one that wanted the baby, and he did not even want any more kids.

- When his dad died I was there for him. I went to the funeral with him. I went to his family members house with him the day they found out his dad died. I bought him some liquor, cigarettes, jerk chicken, and gave him the money for some weed the next day. I was also paying him rent at this time $400 a month, I was paying the light bill on the top floor, he was not working yet so I was buying all our daughter diapers, wipes, all the stuff we needed for the house, etc. at the time. One day he made a comment and said I wasn't there for him when his dad died and that the only person that was there for him when his dad died was his cousin because she would come randomly drop him off $100 knowing he needed it. Besides the rent and the gifts, I was giving him and just being there for him he felt I should have been giving him money just because. At this time, I was only making $10 an hour and I was the only one working in the house and he expected me to give him basically everything I had. He never acknowledged the stuff I did do for him he only acknowledged what I was not doing for him. He was never grateful.

- When I first moved I made a contract for him to sign every month with the amount and date I paid him for rent for I could have records if I ever needed it. He complained and signed it, but he kept asking why we would need a contract if we are in a relationship and I was going to pay. I explained that it's better to have everything documented just in case. I went to school for criminal justice, have experience working in a law office and all I watch is court shows so I know how important it is to have things in writing. So, when I took out those two loans to pay the cost of redemption for the property taxes to save his house, I wrote out a contract saying we would both split the monthly payments equally for the two loans, I would put the gas, Wi-Fi and light bill in my name and we would split the payments and I would not have to pay him rent anymore. He got really offended that I wanted him to sign the contract and refused to sign and said "IF THAT'S WHAT WE AGREE ON WHY DO I NEED TO SIGN THIS? ALL THE STUFF GO BE IN YO NAME ANYWAY. YOU GO GET YO MONEY. YOU JUST WANT A REASON TO TAKE SOMEBODY ON ONE OF THEM DUMB ASS COURT SHOWS" what he said made no sense because if he planned on paying then why would I have a reason to sue him? The contract was protecting us both just in case. He refused to sign it, but he did stick to the agreement. He was late a couple times on some payments and paid me back when he could. One time he even had the audacity to say "I still think you should be giving me like $200 a month" even though we were splitting all the bill equally and everything was in my name and I just made my credit score go down by even taking out the two loans. He was also making more per hour than me at his job. Even though I did not give him the extra $200 a month, him saying that was showing how manipulative, controlling and financially abusive narcissist can really be.

- Another example of how controlling and manipulative he was, anytime we were on the phone together and I would say I would call him right back. He would never answer after that. Even if I call him right back in like two minutes he would not answer me. I could be out at a store or out running an errand and he would just stop responding and when I get home and ask him why he stop responding he would say "I was just talking to you. You hung up. Do what you were doing when you hung up" If I call him right back in less than five minutes I don't understand what he could be so insecure about. He wanted to control me and manipulate me into thinking that I was wrong for telling him I would call him right back. This did not just happen one time, this happened quite often. To the point where I would have to ignore family members phone calls or other important calls just because I didn't want him to think I was doing something I wasn't supposed to be doing.

- Anytime I would get him a gift no matter how much it costed or how much I sacrificed for it, it was never good enough. I would surprise him with random gifts, money, baskets, weed, drinks, etc. Sometimes he would be like "Why you aint get me [insert something else] too?" and he thought that was okay but to me it showed how ungrateful and unappreciative he really was. But whenever he would give me a gift I always appreciated it no matter how little effort he put into it. I never asked him why he did not get something or complained about anything because I understand that when a person gives you a gift that is something they chose to do and not something they had to do. One time in February I was saying I needed me some new work shoes and I was going to get me some all-black air force ones and he said, "I'll just get them for you for valentines' day" and I was really excited so the day of Valentine's Day he sent me a picture of the shoes and instead of the black air force ones they were some all red air force ones. Red is my favorite color and I really liked the shoes, but it caught me off guard because we talked plenty of times about the black air force ones and they were even on the list I sent him of what I wanted for valentine's day. I did not act ungrateful at all. I gave him a big hug and told him thank you. Two months before that I just bought me some red and white air force ones and I had been talking about needing the black shoes for work, but I didn't say anything because I didn't want to ruin the moment. Out of nowhere he said "I didn't think it would be a big deal getting you red shoes instead of black because you could easily go switch them if you want" that comment right there lets me know he intentionally did this. This is typical narcissist behavior. They do things like this all the time and make it seem like they didn't mean any harm when they really did. If this were the other way around and he sent me a picture of one exact pair of shoes he really wanted and I went to the store and got some other ones and told him it was no big deal he would have had a fit. They constantly do things they would have a problem with if it's being done to them. It was very common for narcissist to ruin holidays and other special occasions. They will purposely try to make these days miserable for you or find any reason to provoke an argument.

- Like I just previously mentioned, It is very common for narcissist to ruin holidays, birthday's, and other special occasions for their spouse. For a small part of my pregnancy, I ended up moving out because he started treating me horrible, but I had already made a doctor's appointment and the doctor's appointment was about five minutes away from his house and it took me about forty minutes to get out there. We got in a small argument (I cannot remember what it was about) and when I got out there he decided not to go to my first ultrasound appointment with me. Even though it was right down the street from his house and I had drove all the way out there. So, I had to go to the appointment by myself and sit in the hospital by myself and do my first ultrasound alone when I really wanted him to be there. He ruined such a special day. He did the same thing when I was in grief counseling after my dad died, it was our last session and we were going to have food and celebrate the end of grief counseling so as I'm on the way to the church where the grief counseling was held at, he calls me with an attitude "WHY DID YOU BREAK MY WASHING MACHINE" and I was so confused asking him what he was talking about because I had not even touched the washing machine that day. Last time I used the washing machine it worked fine. And when I asked him what he was talking about and said I did not touch the washing machine he just hung up in my face and when I called him back he did not answer so my mood is already messed up now and I ended up turning around and going back home and missed the last day of grief counseling because I was so upset that he randomly called me with an attitude claiming I broke the washing machine. When I got home the washing machine was not even broke. He just wanted to ruin the day for me. Most holidays with him there was always an argument. Not matter what he always found a way to make me miserable.

- He expected me to run all his errands for him. No matter how I felt or what I was doing he thought I was supposed to just up and go wherever we wanted me to go. I could be at the house upstairs and he be downstairs, and he would either call me or text me and be like "u on yo way" that was his way of asking was I going to the store or going to get some food or wherever he wanted me to go. And when I would say no I'm not going anywhere he would try and manipulate me and make me feel bad and say "YOU CAN'T NEVER DO SHIT" he had a car and could drive and go to the store himself or go get his own food or cigarettes but when he didn't feel like it he felt it was my duty to run his errands. If he did not have his cigarettes he would get mad and start screaming "I NEED SOME SQUARES!!!!!!!!" It did not matter if I was resting, not feeling well, doing homework or simply just did not feel like it. He only cared about what he wanted. But if it were one of his coworkers that called and wanted him to go somewhere he would jump up out of his sleep for them and leave and not say anything. Or if he were mad at me he would go and run his own errands with no problem but if we were on talking terms he would constantly beg me to go run his errands. Sometimes I would go do it just because I did not want to hear his mouth or sometimes I would go run his errands just to get a break away and have some me time.

- Anytime I would bring up anything regarding another male rather it be a random person, worker at a store, coworker, family member, etc. he would always make these jokes about me being promiscuous and say little things like "that's yo boyfriend" or accuse me of flirting with them but if I dare bring up another woman to him he would instantly get defensive and start saying I'm the cheater and how much he never cheated and he want to give me a reason to feel insecure so bad. I can admit to my wrongs, but he acted as if he was not entertaining other women and that he never cheated on me which I found out was a lie.

- There were plenty of times he would act like he was going to work but really was not going to work. Some of the times I would not even say anything, and I would just let him live his lie but when I would mention it he would get defensive and start screaming and calling me out my name. He would accuse me of lying to him about going to work but I can honestly say I never told him I was going to work and then did not go to work. There would be times I would get off an hour or two early because my boss would let me leave early because it was a slow day, or I would have to leave early and pick up my daughter and anytime I left work early I would go straight home. He would lie about going to work and come home a couple hours later drunk or he would lie about going to work and really be going to hotels with his coworker/side chick. He would even slip up and say how one week he only worked one day but that same day he left out three times supposedly going to work. He would often tell on himself and not even realize it. Or he would claim he worked an entire week and then when he got paid he would be complaining the next day about how he did not have any money.

- One of the girls he had sex with before me would often pop up at the house out of nowhere. He claimed that she was obsessed with him and would find any excuse to pop up at the house. He said every time she would come around she would try to get him to have sex with her, but he would always turn her down. One day I saw a text she sent him a couple days before our daughter was born she sent told him to text her the address because she was getting a ride there. I thought this was very strange because he wasn't selling weed anymore so it's not like she was trying to buy some weed from him. He told me before that he knew she still wanted him but he would always turn her down so I don't understand why would you keep entertaining this woman knowing she want you and letting her come to the house when I'm at work? All I wanted to know was what was the purpose of her coming over and when I asked him he got really defensive screaming "I DIDN'T FUCK HER. THAT'S ALL THAT MATTERS" he never said the reason she came over and didn't think there was anything suspicious about any of this especially when I blocked her before from his phone and suddenly she was unblocked. But if it were me entertaining a man I used to mess with, and he kept popping up he would have had a big problem with it. Narcissist can never see the wrong in their actions, only yours.

- There was a girl that he had sex with over 10 years ago and he was still friends with her and one day while him and I were in a relationship she sent him some naked pictures of herself. He did not respond to it but when I brought it up to him he claimed she was "just a thot that was feeling herself" but I thought it was inappropriate for her to be sending him those kinds of pictures when he was in a relationship. She clearly felt comfortable sending the pictures to him. He would only talk to her when I wasn't around. She would text him flirty things like "you want to smoke lil ugly" and I overheard him telling someone one day that even though he had not had sex with her in over ten years, in summer 2017 she was horny and ready but (the girl I mentioned in the previous post) ran her off. One time when I moved out he sat on the phone with her for 1 hour and 18 minutes but when I was in the home he never talked to her. The entire situation was suspicious to me because if the roles were reversed and it was me that had a guy friend sending me naked pictures and flirty text and I only talked to him when my spouse was not around then he wouldn't like it either.

- When he finally got his job, he would try to talk down on me as if he were better than me and as if his job was better than mines. Before I begged him and convinced him to get a job he was selling weed and begging women, friends, and family for money. When he got his job, he would try to tell me that I do not do anything at my job and that all I do is text him. I was working in a law office so my job was very important. The difference between my job and his job, I sat at a desk and did work on a computer and sometimes I would have to leave out and run errands like go to the courthouse or go to the post office, etc. There would be down time I would have between working on cases so yes I was able to look at my phone sometimes and text message, but he felt because I was not on my feet all day at work like him then he thought he could talk down on my job. The same job that was supporting him before he started working and while I was pregnant with his child and even after he started working because all his money went to cigarettes, weed, liquor and fast food.

- A lot of times in the relationship when I would complain about something that was not him or his behavior he would act like it's not a big deal and then complain about the same exact thing himself. This happened quite often. If I complained about something it was no big deal but if he complained about the same thing I complained about then it was okay for him to voice his opinion and frustrations.

- Narcissist love to make your life difficult and give you a hard time. They don't want peace. They love drama. I noticed many times in the relationship when I or someone else would buy him something and ask him the size or he say what size he wore; it would always be the wrong size or be too small. At first I thought this was a simple mistake but once I saw this happening at least five different times and I noticed the pattern I realized he was doing this intentionally. And I mentioned this before to him and he got defensive as usual and said why would he tell somebody the wrong size if they are doing something for him? Which would be a question anybody would want to know but when you do your research on people with narcissist personality disorder, they do things like this. They do it to give you a hard time and inconvenience you. They get a thrill out of giving others a hard time.

- During the last couple months of our relationship, I started buying books on narcissism and how to deal with narcissist and I also had other books too. One day he noticed my large book collection and said "all those books, you know what I could have brought with that money" I did not say anything because if I did he would have got offended and defensive and it would have either been an argument or him giving me the silent treatment but that was so pathetic of him. Instead of worrying about my book collection he should have been adding up all those empty cigarette packs and empty liquor bottles and imaging what he could have did with that money. Anything I had he wanted to know the price of it or even if I had a gift from someone he wanted to know how much they paid for it. He was constantly worrying about my stuff and my money instead of focusing on his own stuff and money.

- Sometimes he would do nice things but usually when narcissist do nice things it's because they have a hidden agenda. If he did something nice like buy me food it was because he expected something in return later. One day he bought me some wings from this place he liked and the next day it was the rapper Pop Smoke's birthday (R.I.P.) and he told me that he was on the phone with one of his male friends and he said he told them that he hopes I buy him a drink that day for Pop Smoke's birthday because he fed me yesterday. I don't see how him buying me 6 wings meant that I should buy him some liquor the next day for Pop Smoke's birthday. We were living together and as a family and raising our child together so there have been times when I would buy us something to eat just like there have been times when he bought us something to eat. When I did it, it was because I was feeding my man and our family but when he did it, it was because he wanted something in return from it. He tried to manipulate me and get me to buy him a bottle of liquor by telling me about the convo him and his friend had. I never once bought him some food and expected something from him the next day. He did not even know Pop Smoke and didn't even know who he was until after he died when one of his coworkers at work introduced him to Pop Smoke's music. Instead of just saying he wanted a bottle of liquor and wanted to drink, he used Pop Smoke's birthday as an excuse for wanting me to buy him some liquor.

- One day I was making some tacos and as I was cooking the ground beef he came in the kitchen and started staring at me and out of nowhere he started screaming at me "THAT'S NOT HOW YOU DO IT. YOU TRYING TO KILL US" It made me very uncomfortable because I had not even finished yet. I was just getting ready to add the taco seasoning in and before I could do it he started screaming at me telling me that I needed to drain the grease and I had not even got to that part yet. He made me very uncomfortable and started calling me out my name and I ended up just not doing anything. I left the tacos how they were and ended up ordering me something to eat because he ruined the moment. Ever since that day he would not let me cook anything and kept telling me I needed lessons, but he never even gave me a chance. Before I moved in with him I was living on my own and had to cook for myself and also took two years of foods class in high school so I was able to cook basic meals but when you are dealing with a narcissist they will constantly criticize and pick at everything they you do to the point where you are so uncomfortable around them that you don't even want to do things because you are afraid of how they will react or you just don't want to hear their criticism. Another similar situation like this would be one day I was about to wash the dishes and before I could even start washing the dishes he came in the kitchen and just started starring at me. I instantly felt uncomfortable because I knew he was looking for any reason to complain and criticize me, so I waited for him to leave out before I started washing the dishes and as I was waiting, the water was just running on the dishes and he started screaming at me "THAT'S NOT HOW YOU WASH DISHES. JUST STOP" I had not even started washing the dishes yet, but he started complaining anyway. He complained about anything I did which made me not even want to do things around him because there was always negativity coming from him.

Those are just a few things I went through while I was in a relationship with the narcissist. There are many others that I did not even mention but all very similar when it comes to the different types of abuse and manipulation tactics you will experience when you are in a relationship with a covert narcissist. It never gets better. They get worse as they get older. You will start to blame yourself and try to figure what you did wrong. Just remember that the best thing you can do is leave. You need to remember there is nothing you could have done to change the outcome of the relationship. They repeat this same cycle with all their victims. They will start off so sweet and charming and you will think you found your soul mate but as time goes in you realize they are not who you thought they were. You will soon realize the person you thought you knew never really existed.

"I think the only ones who could understand this type of abuse is other people who have gone through it. Because if it did not happen to me, I would have never accurately understood it. It feels earth shattering when the mask comes off, and they are so cold, so cruel almost gruesome at times. It is so difficult to accept that none of it was real. You feel traumatized, and really shaken up. It's like waking up from a bad dream, to a nightmare. Especially if you dealt with a covert narcissist, who appeared so good and humble, even kind, and compassionate, only to find the devil at the other end of the mask. Its so difficult getting used to the depth of their cruelty, and their ice-cold hearts. The shock does not wear off easily. At least it didn't for me." – Maria Consiglio @understandingthenarc

REFERENCES

Lancer, Darlene. "All You Should Know about a Covert Narcissist." Psychology Today, Sussex Publishers, 20 Jan. 2019, www.psychologytoday.com/us/blog/toxic-relationships/201901/all-you-should-know-about-covert-narcissist.

MacKenzie, Jackson. *Psychopath Free: Recovering from Emotionally Abusive Relationships with Narcissists, Sociopaths, and Other Toxic People.* Berkley Books, 2015.

Made in United States
Orlando, FL
21 August 2022

21367081R00036